designed to inspire, create, & release

the wonder of a
WORD

Tiffani Lassiter

Published By:
Jasher Press & Co.
www.jasherpress.com
customerservice@jasherpress.com
1.888.220.2068
P.O. Box 14520
New Bern, NC 28561

Copyright© 2014
Interior Text Design by Pamela S. Almore
Cover Design by Pamela S. Almore

ISBN: 978-0692240908

First Edition
Printed and bound in the United States of America

designed to inspire, create, & release

the wonder of a WORD

Tiffani Lassiter

JASHER PRESS AND CO.

It was Your power that created the Earth
It was Your breath that gave life
It was Your mercy that granted forgiveness
It was Your grace that released unimaginable
blessings
It was Your strength that proved endurance during
the storm
It was Your peace that calmed the winds and
waters
It was Your love that displayed sovereignty above
circumstance
It was Your joy that forced the acknowledgment of
Your peace

W

A mple supply maintaining longevity
B eyond borders only He can cross
U nbalanced scales tipped for your favor
N o question or doubts of its origin
D erived from His Words of promise
A nointed by His grace
N ow my hands are able to grasp
C opious treasures of His design
E xceedingly by His will

A nointed one of God
N urturing faith warrior
G uardian and guide of people to Christ
E ffortless giver of love and self
L ord's gift lowered from heaven

W

B oldly stating and/or speaking
E xpressions of joy, peace
L ove and the
I ntriguing likelihood of
E ternal life
F orgiveness, faithfulness, fruitfulness, and
   favor

C hosen Counselor
H oly Spirit
R ighteous Rock
I mmanuel
S avior, Son of God
T ruth and Trinity

D eclare and decree
E verlasting love
E xceptional wonder
P ure yet powerful

D ivine
E ternally grateful
V ictorious
O verflowing blessings
T ender mercies
I nfinite increase
O mnipotent
N othing withheld

W

D estined for greatness
E ncouraged to strive high
T riumphant over circumstance
E xposure to new beginnings
R evived with fierce fire
M anifesting my purpose
I gniting positive change
N egativity not an option
A ccepting the challenge
T hankful for opportunities
I nspired to achieve
O vercomer and conqueror
N o limit attitude

LYRICS OF LIFE

The struggle is over
For the battle was never mine
My inner spirit whispered, take me to the King
It was there I learned that the blood will never lose its power
That God is able
I just need to believe
Lord, I trust You so I'll hold on
You sometimes allow circumstances in order to show Your power
Power to turn it around
You, God are awesome, nobody greater
Today I declare I cried my last tear yesterday
I've been tested, I've gone through the trials, and I've thought I was losing but...
It could be worse
You are my strength and my hope, You brought me out
I will leap into my destiny because I know
My greater is coming

W

E ase the pain
N egativity diminishing
C onscious efforts to uplift
O pening minds and hearts to receive better
U nderstanding it's not on our time
R ealizing a change is inevitable
A ffirming words are spoken into existence
G rateful for second chances
E ndurance strengthens you for victory

Trust the Lord with all thine heart and lean not unto thine own understanding
Make me whole again
Heal me of all that is broken
Clear my mind of weary thoughts left unspoken
Dry my eyes of free falling tears
Your will, Your way, I should have no fears
This journey was of Your own design
Your promise and my faith must realign
I will cry unto God Most High; unto God that performeth all things for me
Praying, trusting that once more joy I will see and peace will be

W

To love You is to trust You
To trust You is to believe You
To believe You is to wait on You
To wait on You is to have patience
To have patience is to endure without complaint

He sees, He hears, He knows
He sees your tears
He hears your cries
It's his gentleness you feel when wiping your eyes
He knows your pain
He's in your heart
He designed the middle and ending from the start

W

Many don't know your story or your struggle
Most don't know your tears or your pain
Few could travel this journey and still remain sane
There may be times when you ask why
The answer only exists in heaven's sky
I applaud and admire your strength and courage
You are truly a God sent angel in this earthly place
May you be blessed by His mercy and grace

Please do not continue to weep
Only now do I have my most peaceful sleep
The last breath taken on earth is simply my
heavenly rebirth
Free from struggles, stress and pain
Rejoicing in everything God promised I would
gain
Please do not cry
Today and forevermore I'm flying high
Only gone from your side, not your heart
God has granted a brand new start
Be strong for me, hear the angels sing
Never forget that you are the wind beneath my
wings

W

Diagnosis Doesn't Dictate Destiny

C oping with the pressure,
   treatment and challenges
A cknowledging His healing
   power but accepting His will
N ot wasting a moment, never
   giving up
C limbing an uphill battle
   armed with faith and prayer
E ncouraged by His promises
   of love and life
R e covery and remission await
   at the end of the fight

F irmly planted
A pplying belief
I dentifying with illustrated promises
T rusting continually
H is word is true

F orward movements
O bstacles eliminated
R enewed strength, mind and heart
G ladly releasing the bitterness that bound
   me
I ndividual self imprisonment
V acating my sentence because no one
   else is suffering
E normous weights lifted
N egativity no more
E ssence of my being restored
S uccessful journey of soul searching
S piritual healing

W

G olden paved roads of heaven
O pen to all who believe in
D rawing closer to thee

G od glorified
R esurrected Redeemer
E verlasting Father
A lpha and Omega
T he way, the truth, and the life

W

H urt by the one you tru sted most?
E xpect to overcome
A cknowledge His love and grace
L ift yourself in prayer
I magine promises fulfilled
N ever lose your faith
G reater is coming

I am a child of God
I am loved
I am strong
I am blessed
I am flawed yet
I am perfectly designed
I am not immune to trials or tribulations but
I am and will be victorious

W

J esus
E verlasting God
H igh Priest
O nly begotten son
V ine (The)
A bbah
H oly Ghost

J ust to feel You smiling down on me
O utward extension of Your arms to hold
   me
Y esterday, tomorrow and forevermore

W

K indred spirits
I nteracting as one
N ever doubting
G ifts of grace
S igns of an unparalleled power

L istening and hearing one's heart
O bvious connection without conditions
V alidated through words and actions
E lated to experience the emotion

W

M atthew 6:8
A cts 1:7
N umbers 23:19
S am1 2:2 and 12:24
I saiah 65:24
O ld Testament
N umbers 6:24-26

Enter into God's mansion full of promises

Be not ye therefore like unto them
For your Father knoweth what things ye
have need of, before you ask Him
And he said unto them, it is not for you to know
the times or the seasons, which the
Father hath put in his own power
God is not a man, that He should lie neither the son
of man that he should repent, hath
He said and shall He not do it? Or hat He spoken
and shall He not make it good?
There is none holy as the Lord, for there is none
beside thee, neither is there any rock
like our God
Only fear the Lord, and serve him in truth with all
your heart for consider how great
things he hath done for you and it shall come to
pass that before they call, I will answer
and while they are yet speaking, I will hear
The Lord bless thee, and keep thee
The Lord make his face shine upon thee and be
gracious unto thee
The Lord lift up his countenance upon thee, and
give thee peace

W

N eeded and allowed

E ssential for growth both physical and
spiritual

C ircumstances created with intentional
design

E quipping you with the strength and heart
for the test

S eeing your way through the storm

S urrendering to His will

A pplying the written gospel

R ealizing it was all meant for good

Y ou are preparing me for my blessing

O nly God can
M ake a way out of
N o way even
I f it seems there's no
P ossible positive
O utcome, He
T urned it around for our good
E levating us from the fall into the open pit
N ever having left our side
C ount it all joy
E xercising faith in The Almighty

W

P owerful presence to strengthen, heal and uplift
R espected, reverenced and adored
A nointed Son of God
I rreplaceable keeper of my soul
S overeign author of faith
E xhalt and glorify the Most High

P ersonal
R elevant
A ble
Y earning
E xpressive
R eality

W

Q uality
U ninterrupted
I ntimate
E xplorations with
T he Father, The Son, and TheHoly Spirit

R enew my peace
E levate my mind
S trengthen my spirit
T ouch my heart
O rder my steps
R espond in Your timing
A rranged with strategic intention
T ransgressions forgiven
I dentity reclaimed
O bligated to acknowledge
N ever to forget His power

W

S pared and saved
P redestined with a purpose
I nvaluable gift of life
R edeemed by His word
I llustrated by His love
T ouched by an angel

T otal and absolute
R ecognition and respect for the
U nchanging and unmatched
T houghts and works done by
H e that is higher than the highest

The wonder of a WORD

W

U nderstanding
N eighborly
I dentifying with
T ogetherness
E mpathetic
D evoted

She

Whether it be celebration or time of sorrow
She encourages and insists you live a better tomorrow
She shares your biggest joys and feels your deepest pain
Your biggest ray of sunshine despite the pouring rain
She offers a shoulder to cry on, lends a helping hand
She stands close by to pull you out from the quickly sinking sand
A voice of reason speaking honest and true
She is that one who always keeps it real for you
She watches your back , day in and day out
If you haven't already guessed it, your sister is who I'm speaking about
Sisterhood is not only through blood relation
It is a bond created from love and dedication
We stand side by side in different faiths and designs
Connected by a genuine friendship, that mighty tie that binds

A sister will refuse to let another fall
She catches you and says "girl, you know you better stand tall"
What a blessing it is to share that kind of bond
Showing that love each and every day, not waiting until one is gone
Together, reaching, striving, climbing new heights
Near and far I ask, no, I pray that we as sisters unite

V alue of my being measured priceless
I nventory of myself proved worthy
C onfident of my character
T rusting in my God given abilities
O ptimistic about rising above obstacles
R allying across the finish line
Y es I can, I will, and do still win

W

W ake me and I say thank you
O ffering gratitude for countless blessings
R eflecting on Your mercy, grace, and goodness
S inging praises in Your honor
H earing and feeling your presence
I gnite the fire and passions of the heart
P roclaiming true belief and adoration

Y earning for a closer relationship
I magining long walks with you
E mbracing Your Word and promise
L ooking to You for direction
D reaming of new and better days ahead

W

Dreams

Dreams of love and peace
Ending the fighting and wars that will
never be won
Immobilizing hatred and injustice
Keen eyes that see character not sex or color
Dreams
Dreams of a world where there is no hunger
Acknowledging starvation is present here and
abroad
Extending support to those in need
From the goodness of one's heart, not for public
praise or recognition
Dreams
Dreams of children adored and not abused
Our elderly respected and appreciated not
forgotten
Strength in numbers for togetherness
Dreaming into existence
Dreams into reality
Dreams

Every imperfection was designed perfectly

Not in His perfect timing for your life because He loves you that much

The intentional accident

When the lesson is the blessing

Food For Thought

The screams of silence are deafening
When eyesight distorts the vision

Is there a book inside of you? Ever wanted to self publish but didn't know how? Concerned about the financial part of self publishing? Relax. Take a deep breath. We can help!

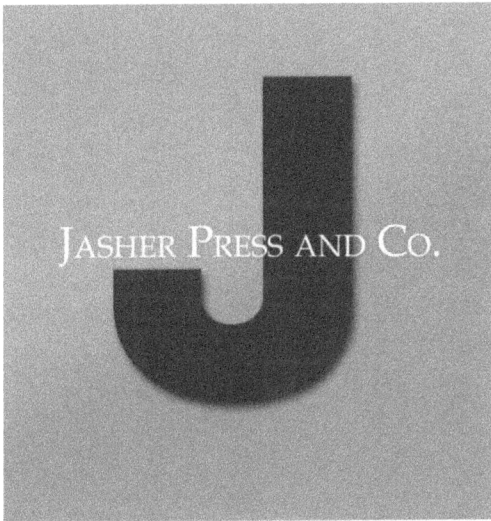

JASHER PRESS AND CO.

Finally! An affordable Self Publishing company for all of your Self Publishing needs. We have the right services, with the right prices with the right quality. So, what are you waiting for?

Unpack those dreams, break out that pen, your dreams of getting published may not be so far off after all!

Jasher Press & Co. is here to provide you with Consulting, Book Formatting, Cover Designs, Editing Services but most importantly inspiration to bring your dreams to past.

And this whole process can be done in less than 90 days! You thought about it, you talked about it but now is the time!